CELEBRATING THE FAMILY NAME OF DUNCAN

Celebrating the Family Name of Duncan

Walter the Educator

Silent King Books
a WhichHead Entertainment Imprint

Copyright © 2024 by Walter the Educator

All rights reserved. No part of this book may be reproduced in any manner whatsoever without written permission except in the case of brief quotations embodied in critical articles and reviews.

First Printing, 2024

Disclaimer

This book is a literary work; the story is not about specific persons, locations, situations, and/or circumstances unless mentioned in a historical context. Any resemblance to real persons, locations, situations, and/or circumstances is coincidental. This book is for entertainment and informational purposes only. The author and publisher offer this information without warranties expressed or implied. No matter the grounds, neither the author nor the publisher will be accountable for any losses, injuries, or other damages caused by the reader's use of this book. The use of this book acknowledges an understanding and acceptance of this disclaimer.

Celebrating the Family Name of Duncan is a memory book that belongs to the Celebrating Family Name Book Series by Walter the Educator. Collect them all and more books at WaltertheEducator.com

USE THE EXTRA SPACE TO DOCUMENT YOUR FAMILY MEMORIES THROUGHOUT THE YEARS

DUNCAN

The name of Duncan, proud and true,

A heritage that breaks the blue.

With roots that spread through land and time,

They rise, they stand, in every climb.

In every heart, a fire ignites,

A legacy that soars to heights.

With strength and courage, never small,

The name of Duncan answers the call.

Through fields they wander, through hills they stride,

With steady hearts and hands open wide.

In every task, in every chore,

They seek to give, to build, to more.

Their journey's marked by grit and grace,

A family bound in time and place.

From dawn to dusk, they stand as one,

Together strong till day is done.

Through every storm, they make their stand,

Their hearts as steady as the land.

With wisdom old and dreams that grow,

The Duncans' strength will always show.

In hands that work and voices clear,

They lift each other year by year.

Through every challenge, every test,

The Duncans always give their best.

Their legacy, a steady stream,

A family bound in hope and dream.

With every step, with every choice,

They sing their name with heartfelt voice.

Through laughter's light, through sorrow's deep,

The Duncans rise, they never sleep.

Their spirit's fierce, their will is strong,

They carry on, they move along.

A name that echoes through the years,

Through trials, joy, and fleeting tears.

The Duncans walk both proud and free,

A legacy for all to see.

So here's to Duncan, bold and bright,

A name that fills the heart with light.

With strength and love, they find their way,

The Duncan flame will always stay.

ABOUT THE CREATOR

Walter the Educator is one of the pseudonyms for Walter Anderson. Formally educated in Chemistry, Business, and Education, he is an educator, an author, a diverse entrepreneur, and he is the son of a disabled war veteran. "Walter the Educator" shares his time between educating and creating. He holds interests and owns several creative projects that entertain, enlighten, enhance, and educate, hoping to inspire and motivate you. Follow, find new works, and stay up to date with Walter the Educator™

at WaltertheEducator.com

Milton Keynes UK
Ingram Content Group UK Ltd.
UKHW021627011224
451755UK00010B/491